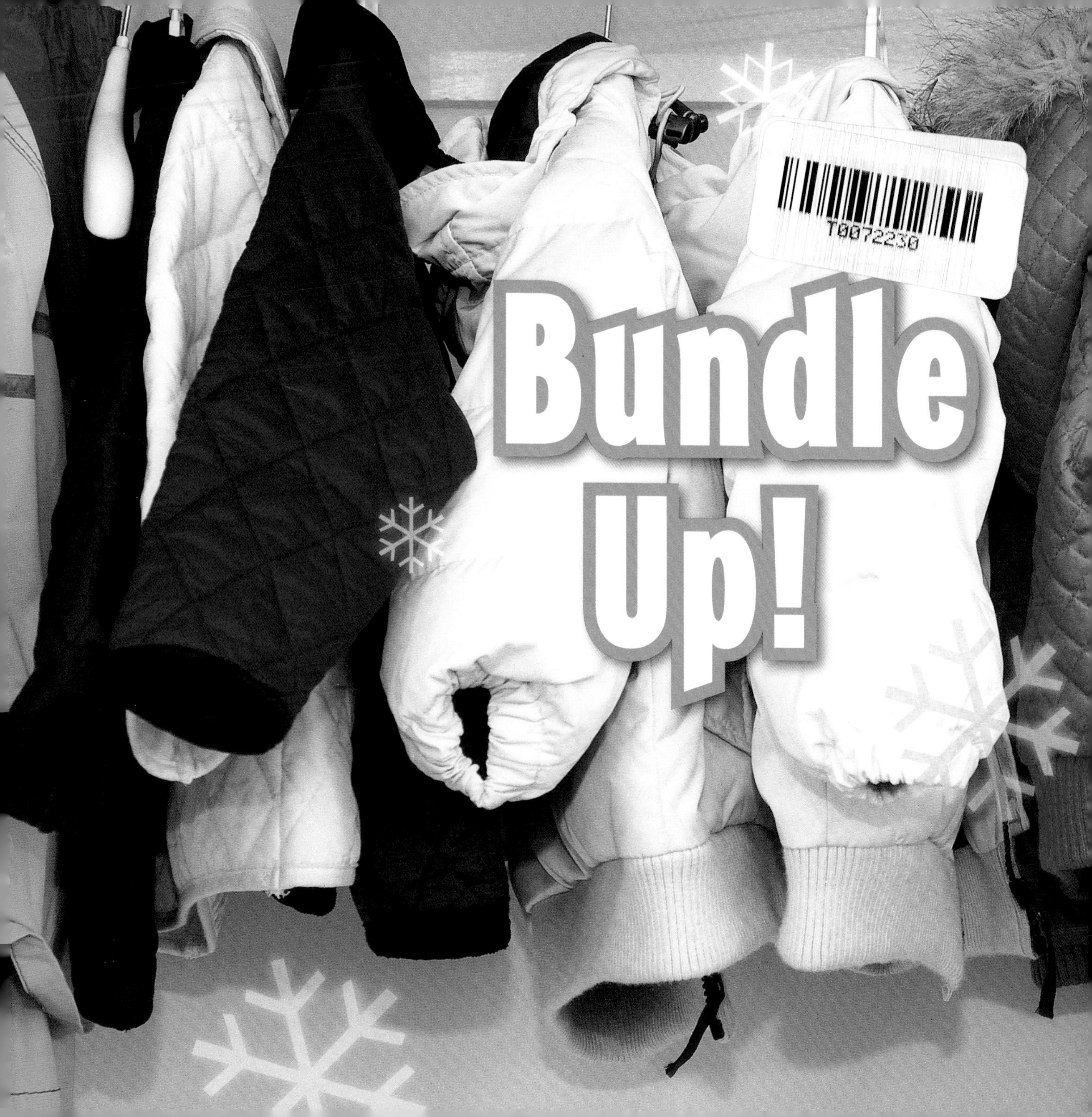

Bundle Up!

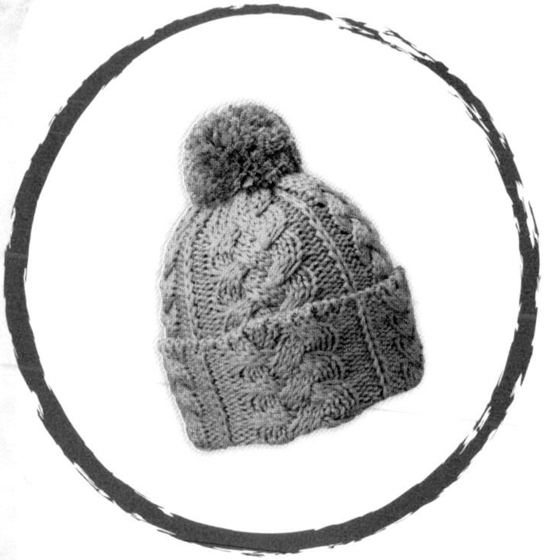

hat

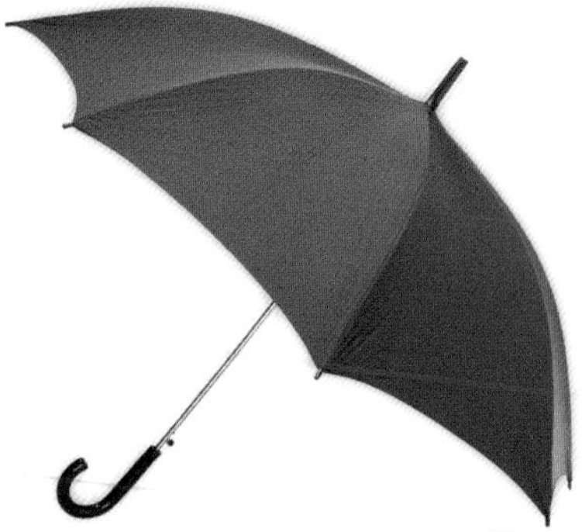

umbrella

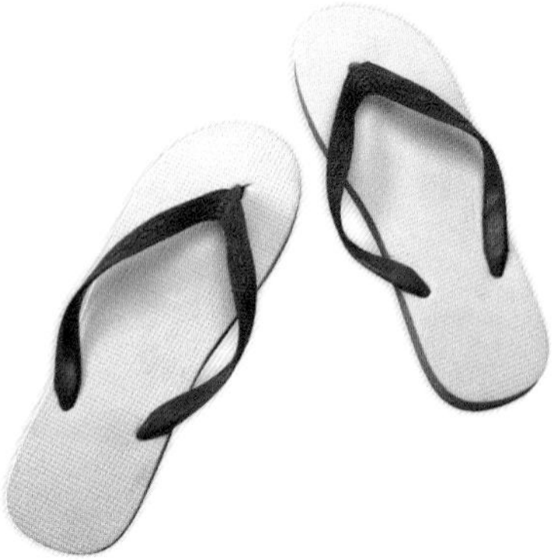

sandals

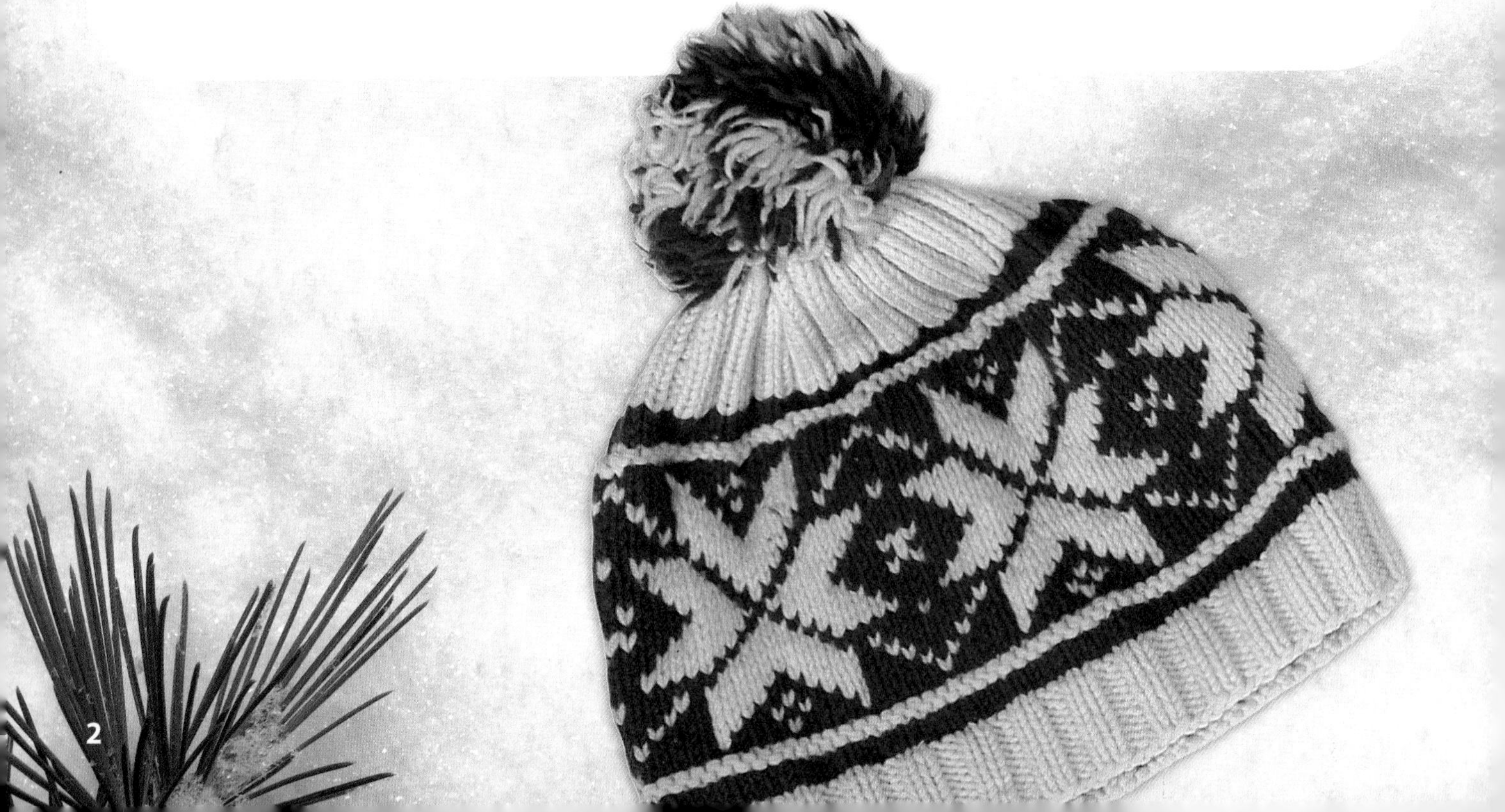

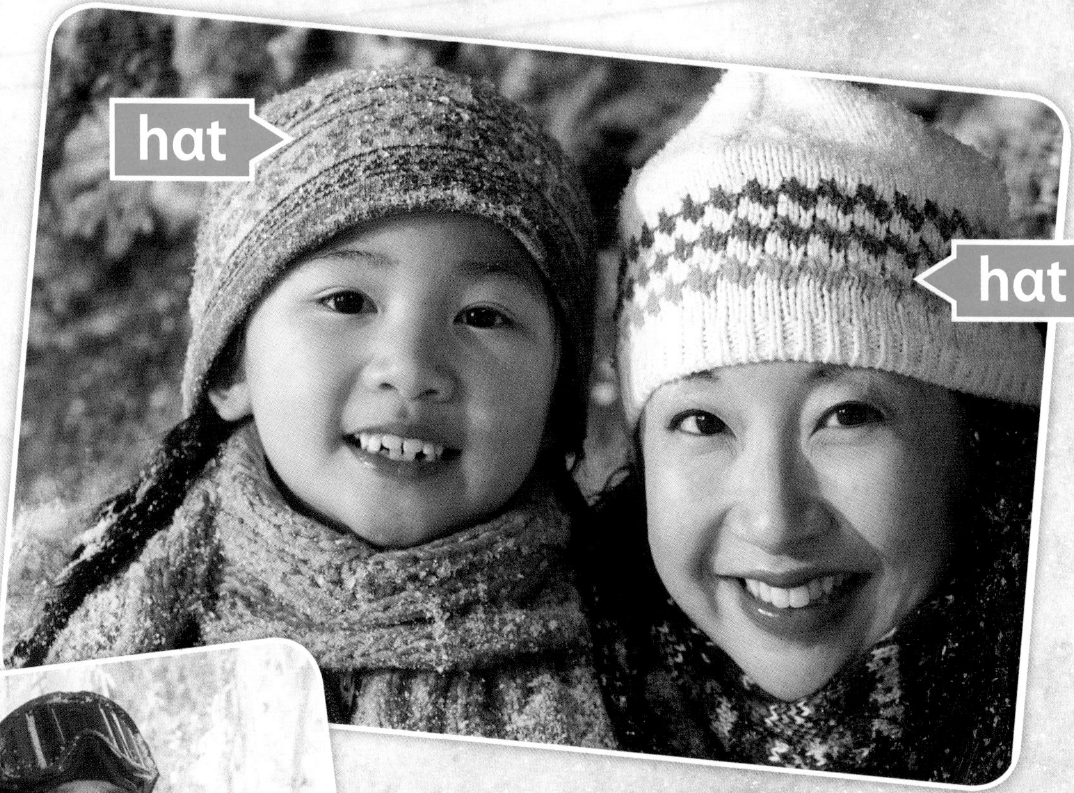
hat
hat

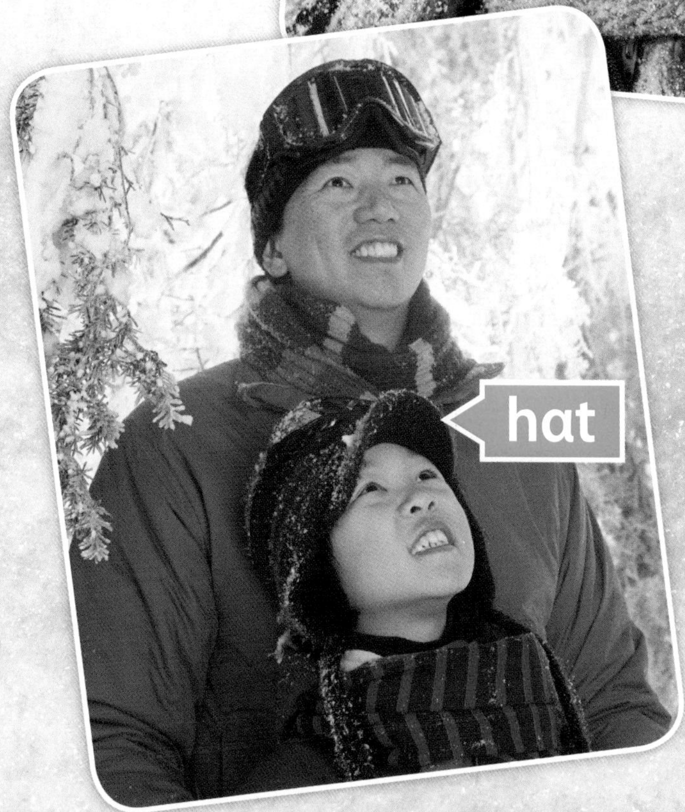
hat

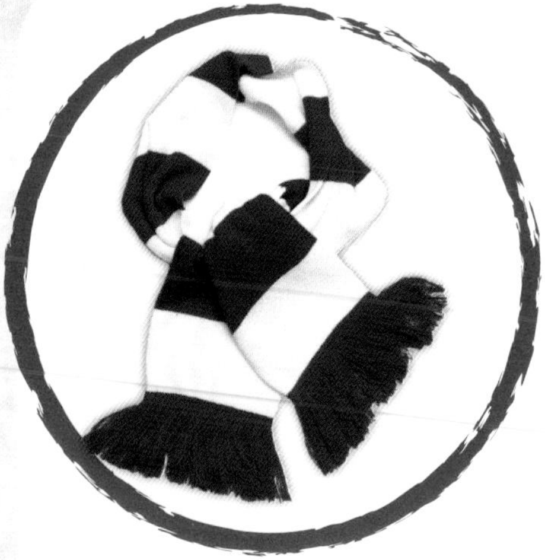

scarf

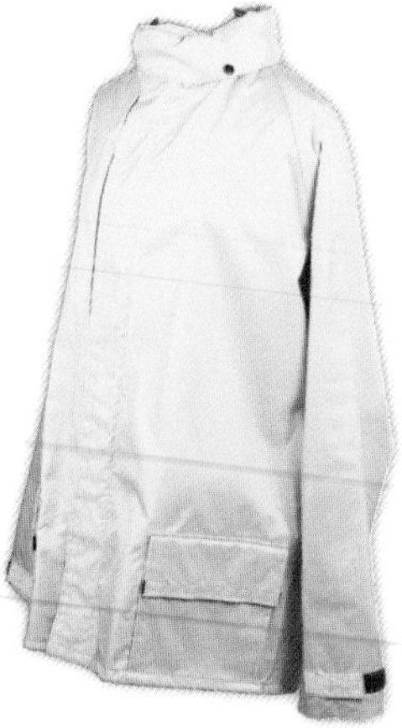

raincoat

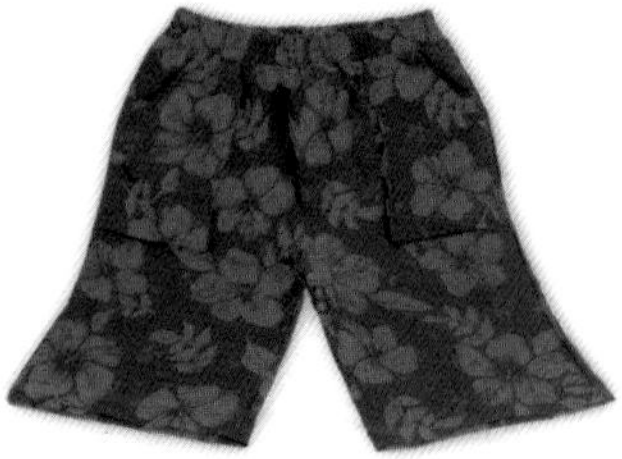

shorts

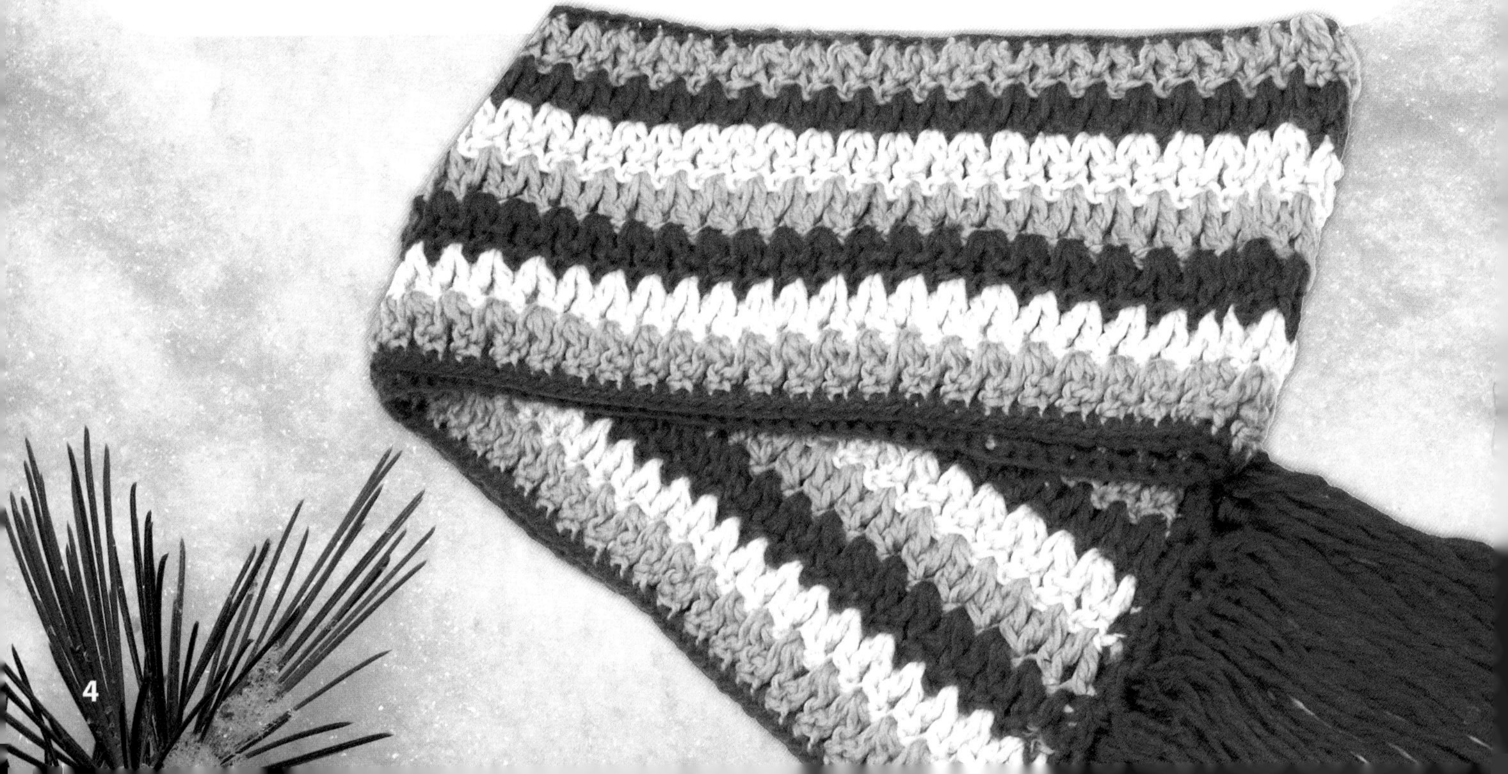

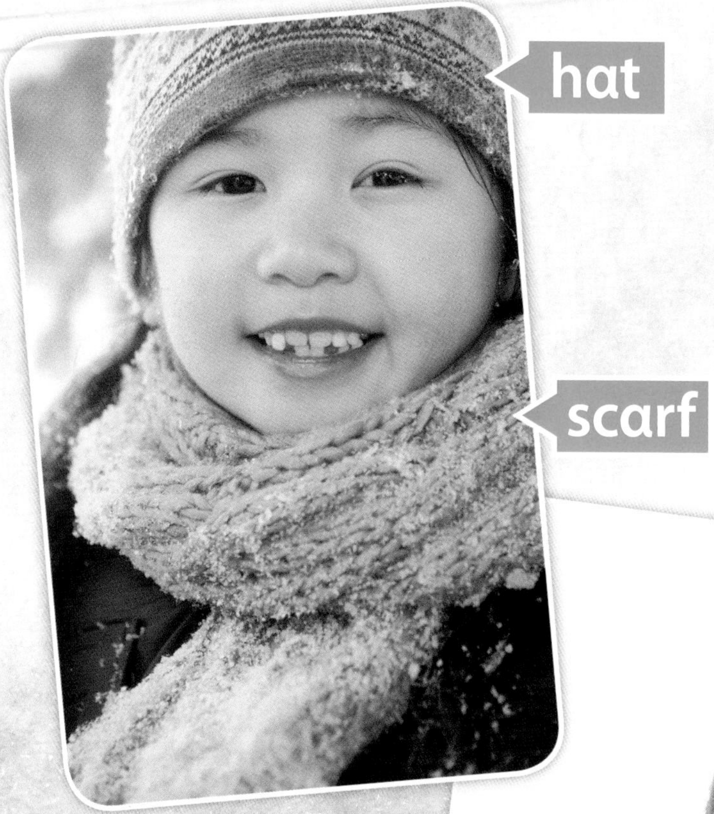
hat
scarf

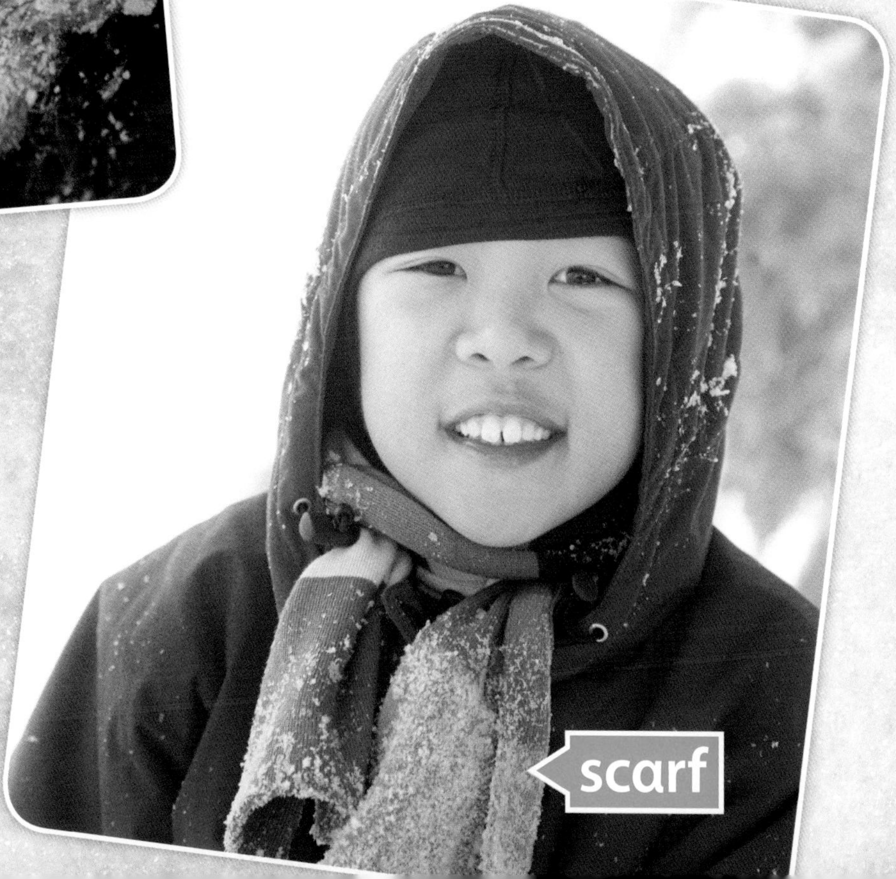
scarf

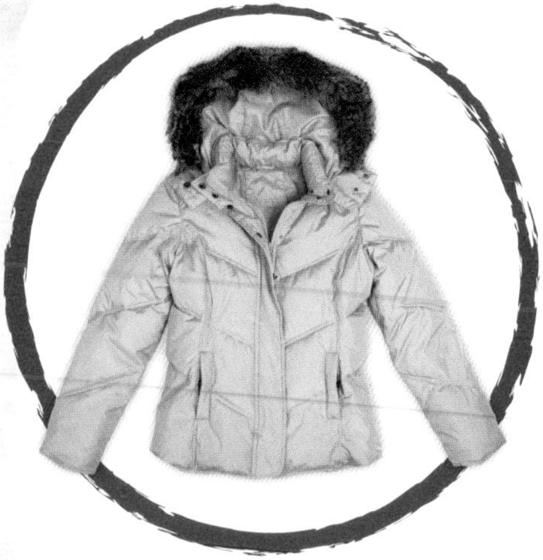

coat

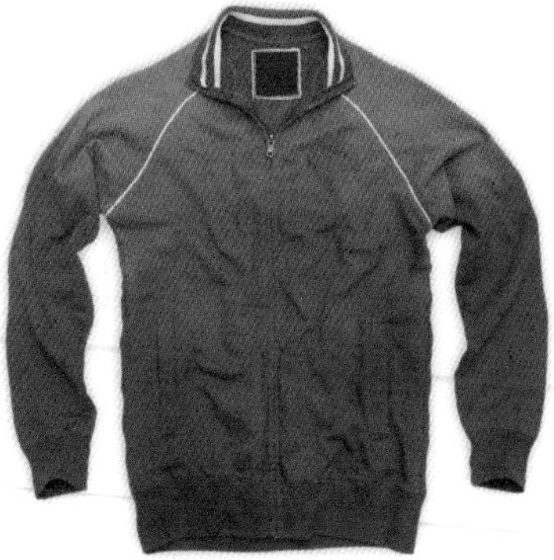

jacket

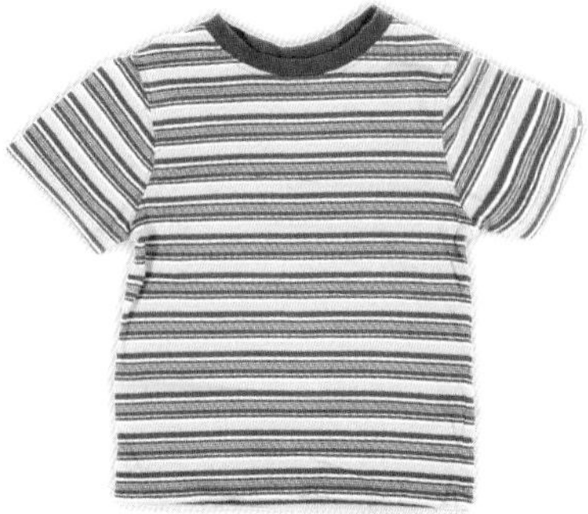

shirt

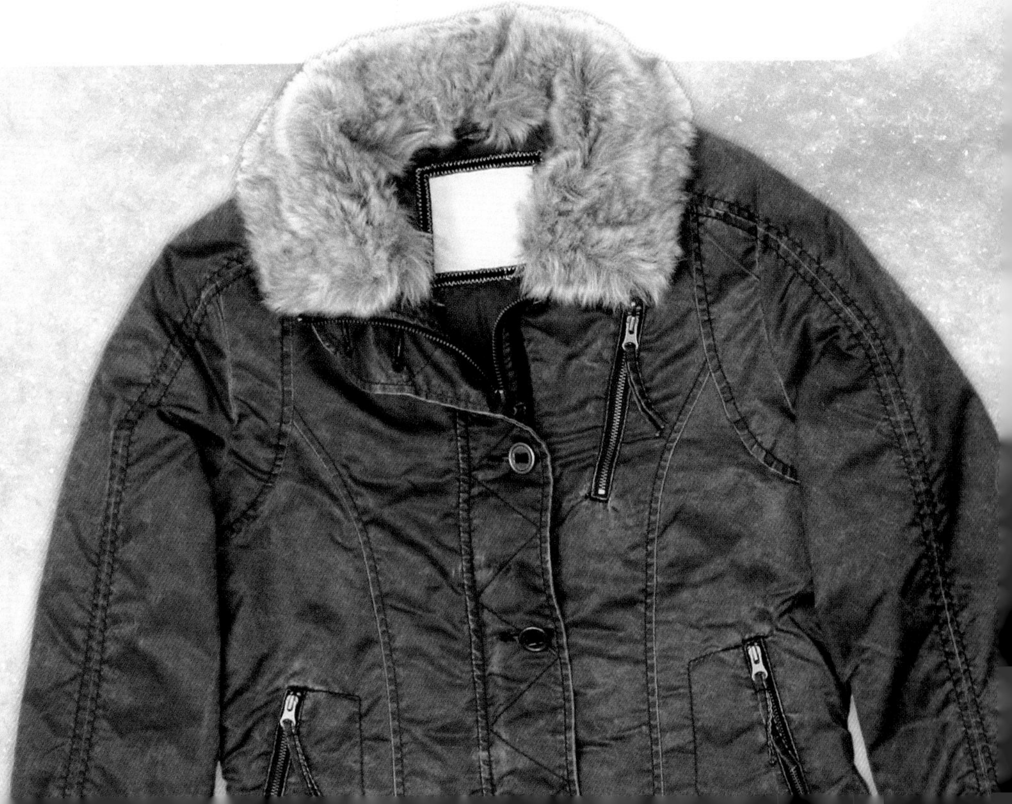

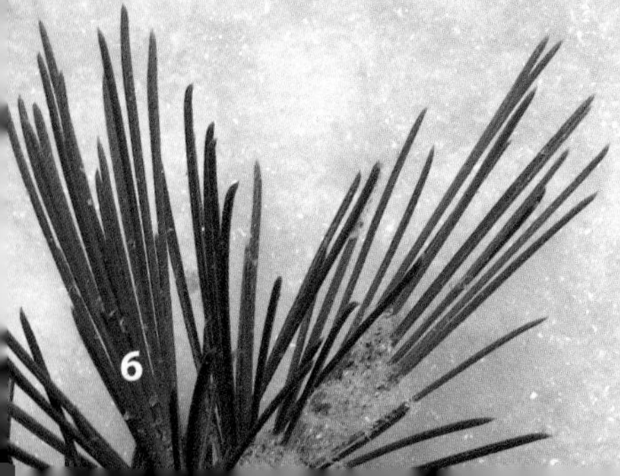

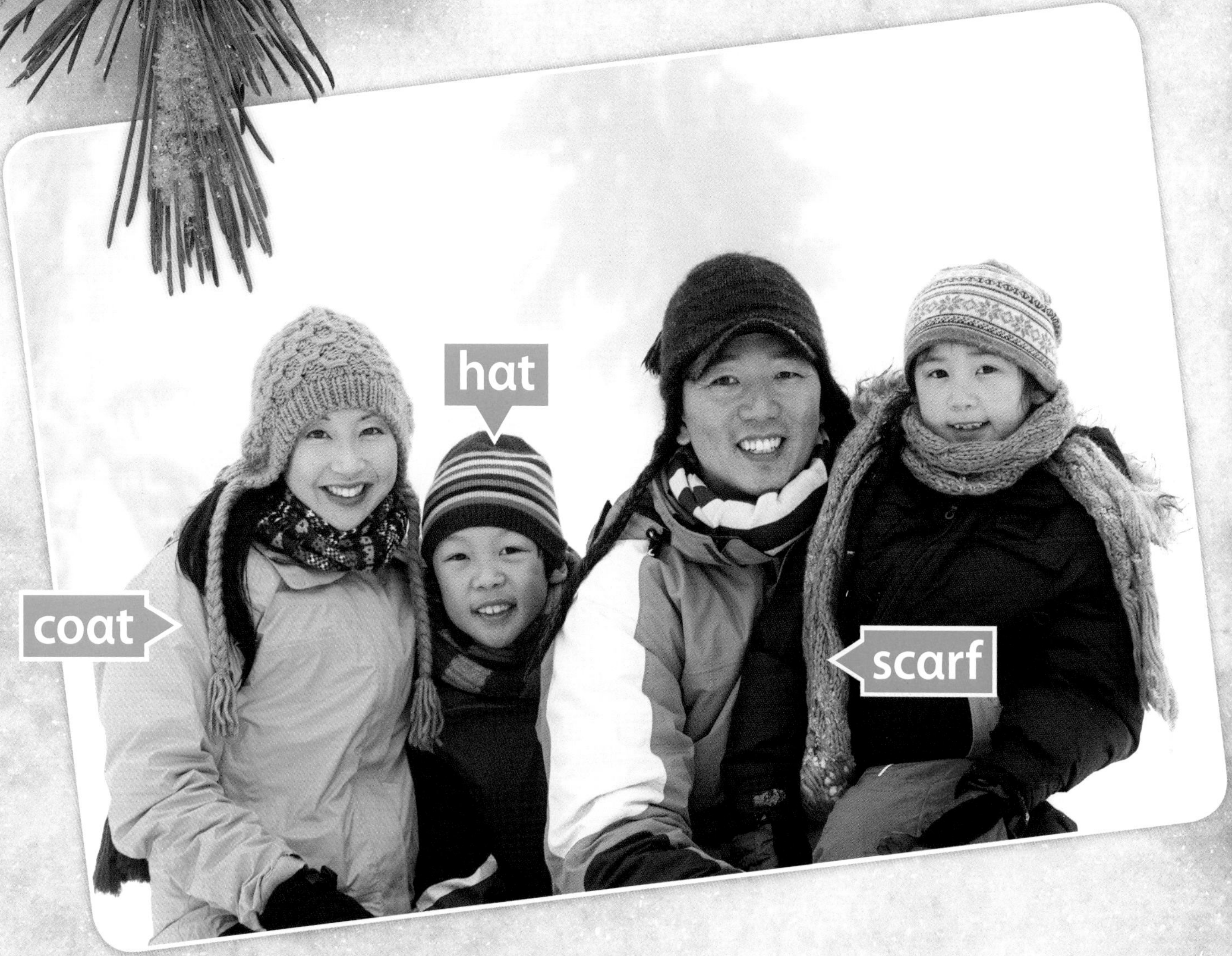
hat
coat
scarf

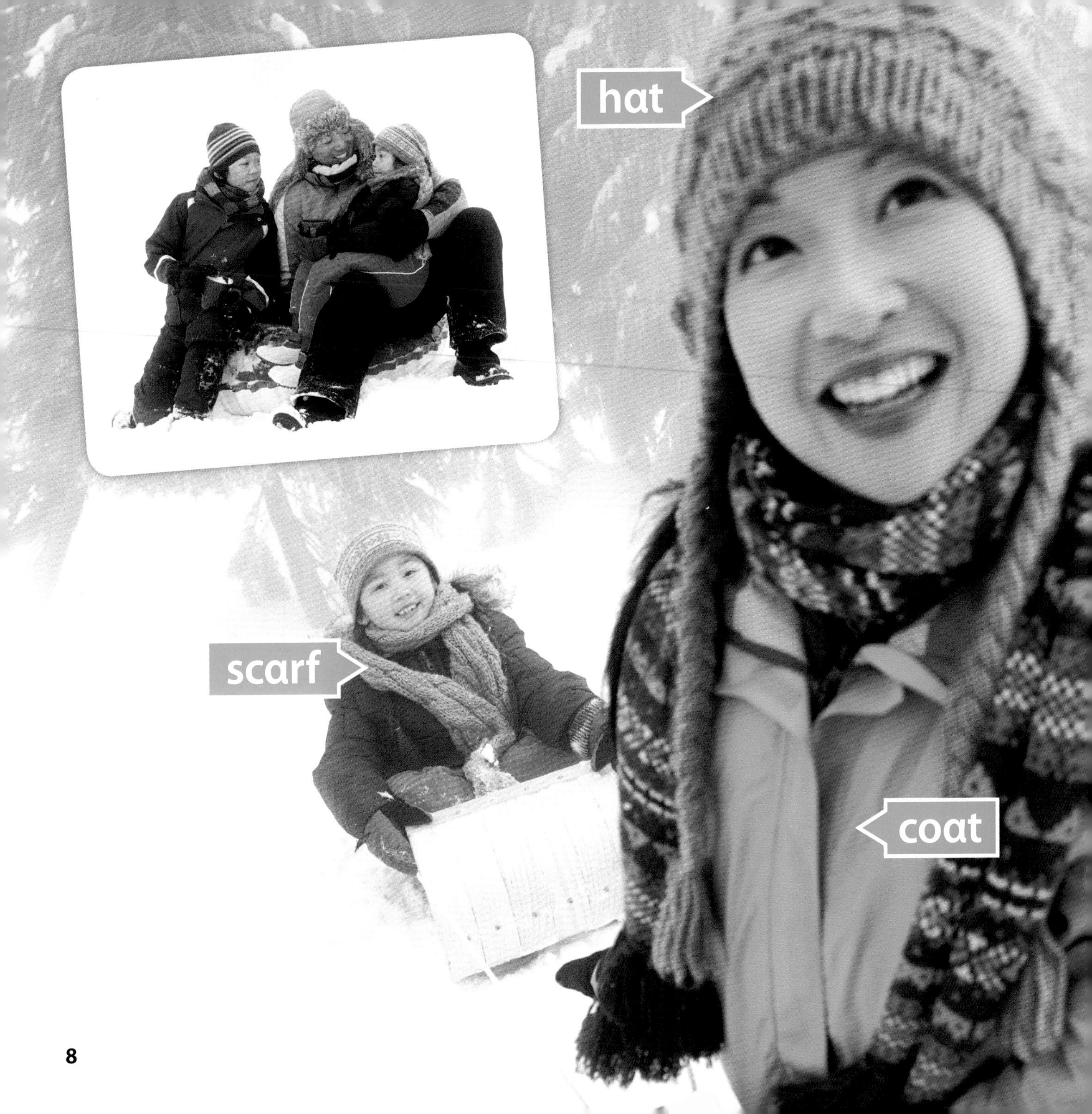
hat
scarf
coat